Published by Creative Education
P.O. Box 227, Mankato, Minnesota 56002
Creative Education is an imprint of
The Creative Company
www.thecreativecompany.us

Design by The Design Lab
Production by Chelsey Luther
Art direction by Rita Marshall
Printed in the United States of America

Photographs by 123rf (Alexander Muntean), Alamy
(Danita Delimont), Dreamstime (Isselee, Liumangtiger,
Ron Sumners), Getty Images (Nada Pecnik, Keren
Su), National Geographic (KATHERINE FENG/
MINDEN PICTURES), Shutterstock (Hung Chung Chih,
iBird, Juhku, worldswildlifewonders), SuperStock
(Minden Pictures)

Library of Congress Cataloging-in-Publication Data
Bodden, Valerie.
Pandas / by Valerie Bodden.
p. cm. — (Amazing animals)
Summary: A basic exploration of the appearance,
behavior, and habitat of pandas, some of Earth's
smallest bears. Also included is a story from folklore
explaining why pandas have black-and-white fur.
Includes bibliographical references and index.
ISBN 978-1-60818-089-9
1. Pandas—Juvenile literature. I. Title.
QL737.C27B627 2013
599.789—dc23   2011050281

First Edition
9 8 7 6 5 4 3 2 1

AMAZING ANIMALS

PANDAS

BY VALERIE BODDEN

CREATIVE EDUCATION

Only about 1,600 pandas live in the wild

A panda is a **mammal**. Pandas are part of the bear family. They are one of the smallest kinds of bear. There are few pandas left in the wild today.

mammal an animal that has hair or fur and feeds its babies with milk

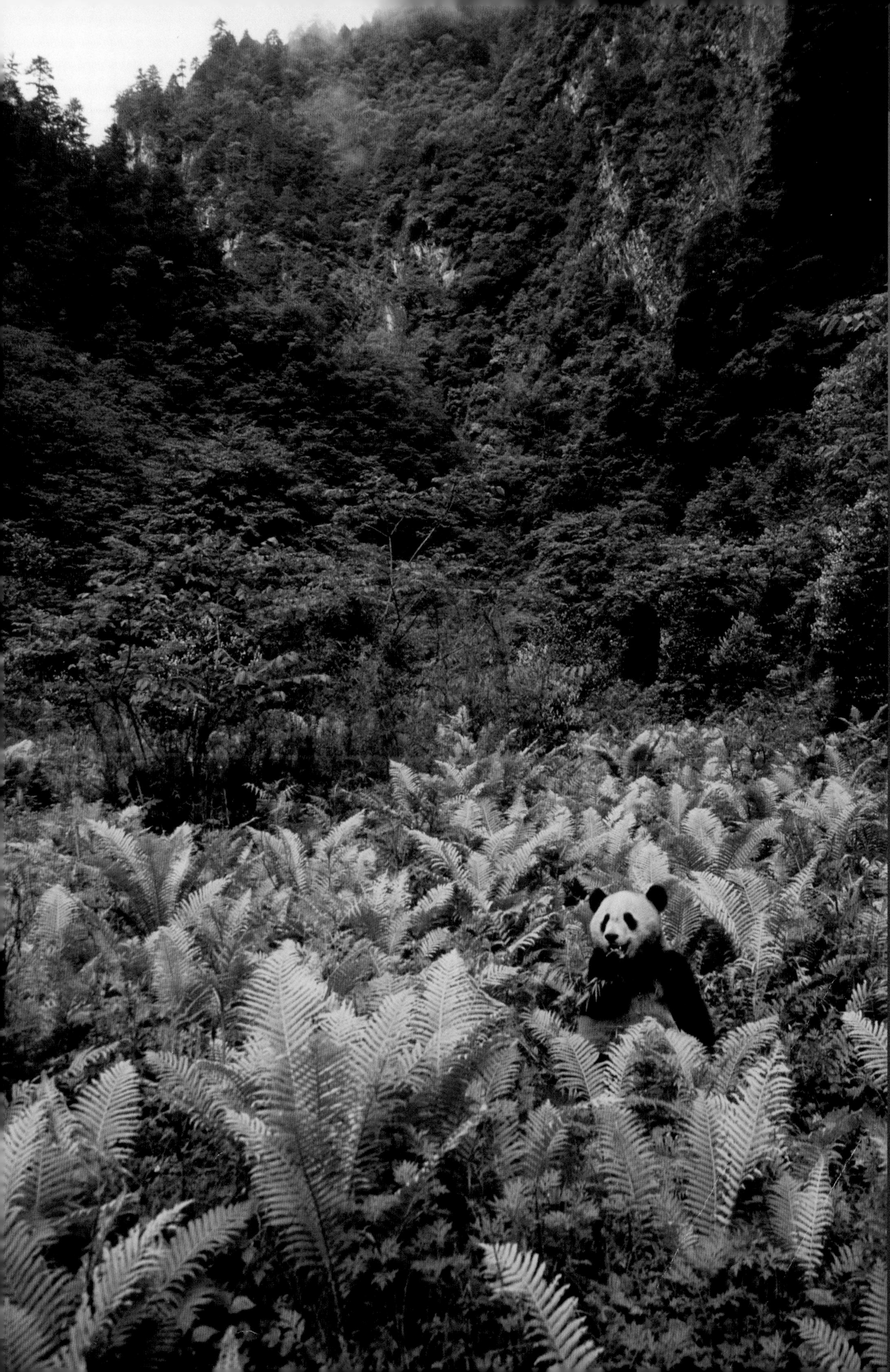

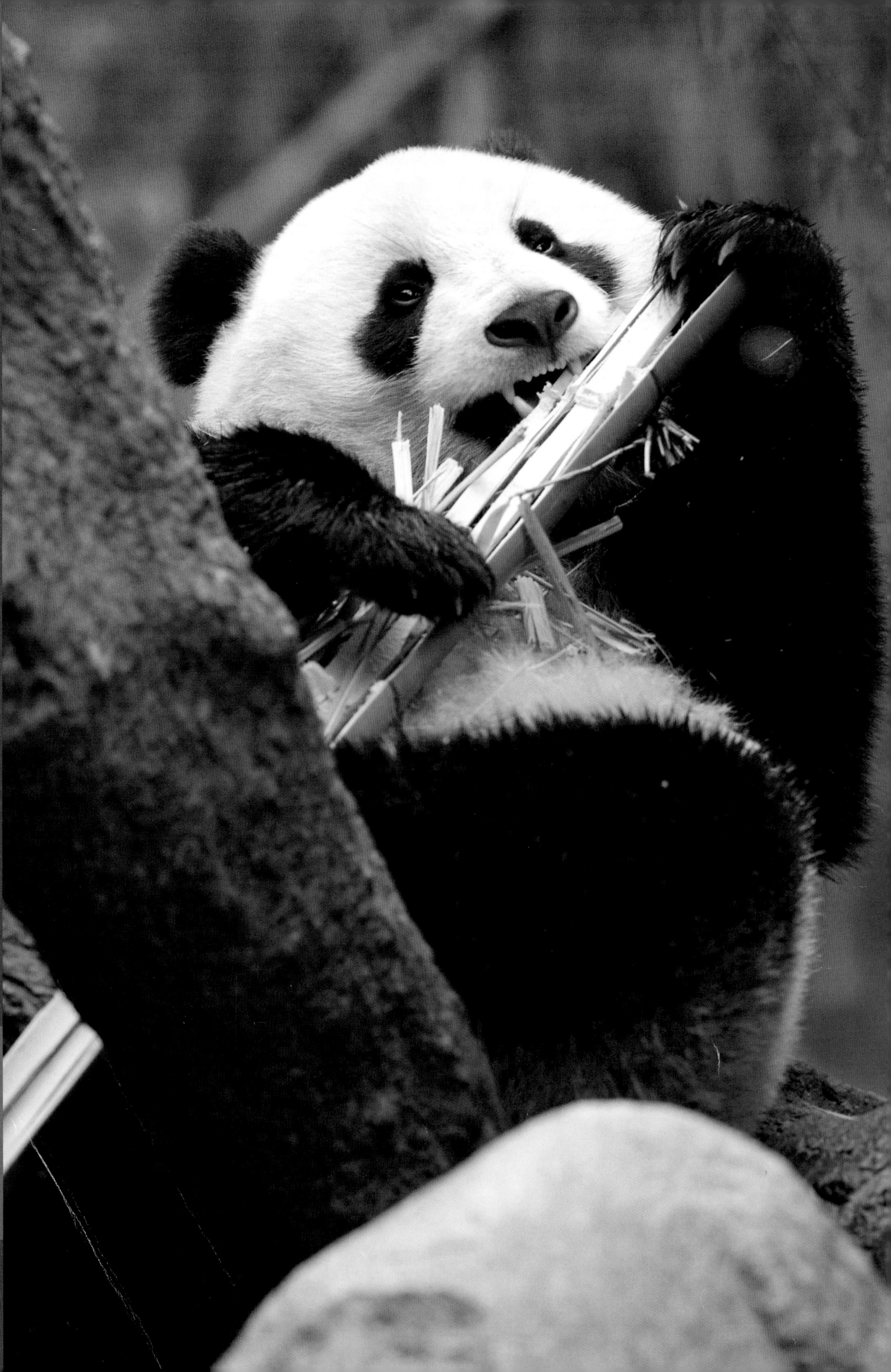

Pandas have thick, black-and-white fur. They have sharp claws and strong legs. Their front paws have a long bone that looks like a thumb. This bone helps pandas pick up things.

A panda's claws and teeth help it to eat woody food

The biggest pandas are about six feet (1.8 m) long. They can weigh up to 240 pounds (109 kg). Female pandas are usually smaller than males.

Pandas are about the size of black bears in America

Pandas live only in the middle of China. They live in bamboo forests there. Bamboo grows on cool, rainy or snowy **mountains**.

mountains   very big hills made of rock

Pandas eat bamboo. Bamboo is a kind of grass that looks like a tree. It has a thick stem, branches, and leaves. Pandas can eat more than 80 pounds (36 kg) of bamboo every day! Once in a while, pandas eat flowers, vines, or even bamboo rats, too.

Bamboo is one of the fastest-growing plants in the world

Female pandas raise their
cubs without any help

A wild female panda gives birth to one or two **cubs** in a **den**. Newborn cubs are tiny. They weigh less than a tube of toothpaste! When a cub is about two years old, it leaves its mother. Young pandas have to watch out for leopards and wild dogs called dholes (*DOLZ*). Wild pandas can live up to 20 years.

cubs baby pandas

den a home that is hidden, like a cave

PANDAS

Adult pandas live alone. They eat bamboo almost all the time. They sometimes eat sitting up with their back against a tree. Pandas nap between meals.

Pandas do not get a lot of energy from the food they eat

Pandas can climb trees. They sometimes roll and play on the ground. Pandas are generally quiet, but they can bark, growl, and squeal.

Young pandas like to play and wrestle with each other

Not many people have seen pandas in the wild. But some people study them at **research centers** in China. Pandas live in zoos around the world, too. It can be fun to see these furry bears up-close!

research centers places where people study something, such as an animal, to learn more about it

A Panda Story

Why are pandas black and white? A story from China says that pandas used to be all white. Then one day, a little girl saved a panda cub from a leopard. The girl died when the leopard attacked her. The pandas were so sad that they pawed the ground and cried. They wiped their eyes with their muddy paws and hugged each other. The mud from their paws left black marks. Pandas have had black-and-white fur ever since.

Read More

Johnson, Jinny. *Giant Panda*. Mankato, Minn.: Smart Apple Media, 2006.

Petty, Kate. *Pandas*. Mankato, Minn.: Stargazer Books, 2005.

Schuetz, Kari. *Giant Pandas*. Minneapolis: Bellwether Media, 2012.

Web Sites

National Geographic Kids Creature Features: Giant Pandas
http://kids.nationalgeographic.com/kids/animals/creaturefeature/panda/
This site has panda facts, pictures, and videos.

San Diego Zoo Panda Cam
http://www.sandiegozoo.org/pandacam/index.html
This site has a live video of pandas at the San Diego Zoo in California.

Index

China 11, 20
claws 7
cubs 15
enemies 15
food 12, 16
forests 11

fur 7, 22
mammals 4
research centers 20
size 8, 15
sounds 19
zoos 20